Everybody Wants to Keep the Moon Inside Them

Everybody Wants to Keep the Moon Inside Them

Ellen Stone

Copyright © 2025 by Ellen Stone

Published by   Mayapple Press
       362 Chestnut Hill Road
       Woodstock, NY 12498
       mayapplepress.com

ISBN 978-1-952781-24-7
Library of Congress Control Number 2025930400

Acknowledgements

Thank you to the following publications where versions of these poems first appeared:

2River; About Place Journal; Anti-Heroin Chic; Arboreal Literary Magazine; Burningword Literary Journal; Cold Mountain Review; Door Is a Jar; Dunes Review; Eastern Iowa Review; From the Waist Down: The Body in Health Care; Great Lakes Review; Heartwood Literary Magazine; Hole in the Head Review; Mantis, A Journal of Poetry, Criticism & Translation; Michigan Quarterly Review Mixtape; Midwest Review; Mom Egg Review; One (Jacar Press)*; One Art; Passages North; Passengers Journal; Philadelphia Stories; Please See Me; Pretty Owl Poetry; Quartet Journal; Rock & Sling: Sooth Swarm Journal; Sweet Lit; Tab: The Journal of Poetry & Poetics; The Maynard; The Museum of Americana; Thimble Lit; Third Coast* (forthcoming)*; Up North Lit,* and, my chapbook, *The Solid Living World* (Michigan Writers Cooperative Press, 2013)

"small map" was nominated for a Pushcart Prize by *Sweet Lit,* 2021; "First married" and "Hunting season" were nominated for *Best of the Net* by *Great Lakes Review,* 2022; "Recipes for mothering" was featured in the exhibit, "Maternal Interior," Ann Arbor Art Center, May-June 2023; and, "In the pond before turning 65" was first runner-up, 2024 *Heartwood Poetry Prize.*

Cover design by Judith Kerman; cover art by Karin Wagner Coron. Photo of author by Jeff Spaulding. Book designed and typeset by Judith Kerman in Calisto MT with cover titles in Book Antiqua.

Contents

A wrist, a wren, a small knife   7

I

Bright side of the moon   11
My life as a jelly jar   13
Cream puffs   14
Perimeters   15
Leftover spools   16
Homemaker   17
Potatoes   18
Mother goes to the underworld   19
Letter to the bedroom window   20
When mother was illusionist   22
Depression as guest   23
House flies   24
Recipe for a daughter leaving   25
Instructions on leaving {mother}   26
The end of childhood   27
Killing the fish   28
Sack dress   29
Girl of prey   30
How to stay alive   31
small map   33
The end of girlhood   34
Hunting season   35
After college   36
Fourth of July   37
How I learned to love Kansas   38
Midwest soil   39
August   40
Planted   41
Argument   42
Cleaning the shed   43

II

Check stubs from the Super Duper   47
Finding shore   48

Container of the world	50
First married	51
River prayer	52
Girth	53
to mother is a strange equation	54
Small jar	56
Restoration	57
Preparing	58
Tethering	59
{plastic}	60
Dissolution	61
Black walnuts	63
Recipes for mothering	64
Snow, the letting go	65
The oldest daughter flies to Dublin	66
Here in the quiet Midwest	67
Daughters leaving home in an age of aggression	68
Late raking	70
Wolf moon over M-14	71
Men I grew up with	72
Coming home: carnival	74
Wolfhound	75
God of dogs	76
How I want the road to you	77
Skating	78
My mother's arms, estuaries at winter's end	79
Her last breath swishes grass	80
In the pond before turning 65	81
About the Author	82
Notes	83
Thank you	84

For my mother, and for my daughters

My Mama moved among the days
like a dreamwalker in a field;
seemed like what she touched was hers
seemed like what touched her couldn't hold,
she got us almost through the high grass…

—Lucille Clifton

She's gone. She was my love, my moon, or more. She chased the chickens out and swept the floor.

—James Wright

Remember: just because you're a daughter doesn't mean you must mend.

—Jihyun Yun

A wrist, a wren, a small knife

After Gerald Stern "Blue Skies, White Breasts, Green Trees"

What I thought was an accordion dangling from an open window
turned out to be man's arm, his shirt sleeve wrinkled in the summer

evening. I thought he was handing me an air pump for my troubles,
instead, he gave me a blank check, pressing it to me with care.

What I thought was a spring bubbling from the hill by the side
of the road was instead a thin blue blazer belonging to a girl.

What I thought were beige high heels lying there were instead
her pearled feet where she lay reading in the fitful weeds.

What I thought was a dark apartment in the city, turned out to be
a church aisle I wandered down. And the baby I thought I saw,

an amberjack floating in a rock basin. What I thought was a couch
to lie on, instead was just a single cushion resting on worn stone.

I thought I heard a bamboo flute wending across the town.
Instead, it was cake batter spun thin inside an olive bowl.

I thought I saw a needle flare in my grandmother's hand.
Instead, it was a bookmark from her bible lying open there.

I thought I saw my brother's jeans hanging on the line.
Instead, it was a roofing nail flashing on the shingles like a gun.

I thought I saw a gazelle loping through the chartreuse corn.
Instead, it was a ladder carved into the horse chestnut tree.

Whatever I was looking for—rust by the railroad, wild oats
sprouting, a boy's hair, peat moss piled for the garden, the way

the mind sponges. My father's sharp trowel I have carried all these
years, a watering can. The tire swing frayed and fallen, the windmill

of my mother's luggage. She was a wrist, a wren in the morning grain,
the scaffolding, elaborate, around her starting to fall. Somewhere

in the haze of my early days, she rose between the geese
and the geraniums, a small knife in her grasp to peel potatoes—

holding the key to our front door that never had a lock.

I

Bright side of the moon

Shining like a lamp holding us all in her steady beam
until there was nothing left, and she went dark. Father

lighting lanterns in the house when the lights went out.
Always walking out a door when he felt like it. Choosing

a destination and roaming even with no light.
While the moon just shines, makes everyone a path.

*

Why did I do so much, Mother wondered at the end.
As if there could have been another way. *Don't use me*

as a role model, I tell my daughters. *Don't do everything
I do*. Working in her shadow—floors clean, dishes swept

off the counter. Don't let the clutter overtake. Mix
and make, mix and make. Skin elastic in the moon.

*

Consumed. *If we had known then,* Father says. As if
we did not know her. As if we did not want to keep

the moon inside us. Swallowed, buttery. We idolize
her, mother, moon—while we are gas or kerosene,

combustible, made solely for consumption. Moon
swelling, overfull, disappearing to the other side.

*

You always look on the bright side, my daughter says
not knowing how much I've searched for her light.

When I was a girl, June blanket of berries to pick
while she was buried in bedclothes, dark clouds.

Scarlet fruit scattered in the garden straw as if
the strawberry moon splintered; I gathered shards.

My life as a jelly jar

When I was newly formed, I gleamed—
        cavorted with the air like some new foal
out in the field, not knowing how to gather yet.

I saw the berries, wild grapes, and yearned to pluck
        but standing only yea high
I did not know what harvest was, nor needed it.

As I grew old, I learned what being filled was like
        and that was all I craved—slick stew of fruit,
its crimson purple hue, and me, subsumed.

As if ripeness began with me, that gloss. Now
        all I want to do is reap. Take
the sweet I muster, preserve it under quilted glass.

But fervor in the kitchen morning, clatter.
        A day is filled with lushness—of girls,
saucy, jamming. Space and corners overflow.

To make and keep, make and keep, a mother's
        adage. Honeyed clamor, tidy shelf.
Eye the ferment, sniff the mash, contain it.

Cream puffs

Those days, she was eggy,
        seemed like the sun always shone,
lemon-sifted spring, lazy
        pollen drifts,
rusted old box grater.

        Stirring vanilla custard, thickened
from just cornstarch, white
        sugar. Dribble thick milk,
yolked in buttercups
        all the live long day. Mom

always cooking something up
        hum, humming.
Drops of batter dough, spun
        with a whack of hands, big
against the faded pastel bowl.

        Nothing matched in the kitchen
but we were clothed & fed enough
        & here come the cream puffs,
bronzed puffballs through
        the splattered oven door,

scotched up against each
        other, sheet-pan steaming.
Let them cool, kids, watch out
        step by the dog. Hack off
the top & slop the cream

        inside. Cloud-sweet fluff—
never let it cool enough, so
        oven warm, & God knows
what we'll have
        for dinner.

Perimeters

After "Kúgha/Home" by Crisosto Apache

We ate our hearts like beets, burgundy juice staining us
until we slipped out some opening while Mom somehow

wound upstairs to bed for good, undone spool of thread.
Only wind hemmed us in—open doors, windows,

hill—solemn bell ringing us clean, storm drenched.
My girlhood periphery—hemlocks first edging

fields surrounded like a cloth napkin laid
whole, Granny's grey shingles, doorstop, lop-

sided plot, brown barn slope, bluestone foot-
prints headed down. Up the asphalt road

swallowed in alfalfa, timothy, orchard glower
fringed with corn, our stucco farmhouse—

chestnut floors with a diamond lookout on top.
We were taught stomach as place, so gutted bull-

heads, rabbits, grey squirrels in the sink, white-
tailed deer tied to rafters, maple trees. Tomatoes, tall

as small ships in the garden dirt, filled canners, cukes
to their jars, vinegar permeating chinks in the old lathe.

Edges then defined us, what perimeters our lives took—
long dirt bus rides, miles walked to town to see a friend.

We worked in nearby haymows, damp milkhouses,
or the ice cream stand on Route 6 over the mountain

walking, always walking away though we were bound
to home like a hound dog that remembers who feeds it.

Leftover spools

In a room made of web, we children spun gossamer thread
shaping space geometrically—turning air into pockets,

cubby holes, more & more intricate until we were trapped
inside corners right in the middle of nowhere, not knowing

our intent to be lost there. Cocooned as any bundled
hominid must feel, so tired & ready for winter to just be done.

Only a child would readily wish to be wrapped in silk.
Woven tightly, a spider's maze while she hummed nearby.

This is when life made sense. When Dad, after work, gutted
squirrel for dinner & grease in the iron frying pan meant

he had provided. No wonder I long for clutter & blank space
brings a case of nerves. Emptiness might mean we'd starve

to death. All that webbing might be claustrophobic, maybe
complicating escape. But nowhere is where we wanted to go.

Homemaker

Dawn and the sun
like a lost child comes back
through the dense trees, triumphant
as if you were wrong about what
would happen if she did not listen.

The only summer sound—a clock beating,
dog's woofs, carpenters nailing a skeletal
frame of a house, lone station wagon, white
and ghostly drifting down the dirt road,
Father asks, "What have you accomplished?"
breakfast things undone, the bread wrapper
lying about like a slovenly house guest.

You are not writing sermons, it is true, nor
spraying the fruit trees, fleaing the hounds,
driving to the town hardware store for screws.
But look how the refrigerator hums in the light
of day like a satisfied customer. The smooth
gleam of the wiped table. How could you ever

stop putting things to rights? The pine cupboards,
a tiny world of their own. Inside, the blue
rimmed bowls nest inside each other, symmetrical
and silent. No one knows how to preserve the world
you have created, but you, your large-veined hands
wringing the damp dish cloth over again.

Potatoes

The milky disc
she handed me
for supper's pot
tasted like
I thought
the moon should
shining through
the front yard pine—
crisp when I bit it
but also, watery
with a touch of salt.
Moons she put
in our soup with milk
and just the smallest
lumps of fried salt pork
and later, tiny pats
of butter floated
on the soup's warm top.

Mom's potatoes—
scrubbed and peeled,
mashed, boiled, scalloped,
fried, baked and hashed—
knobby tubers we
scooped each night
from the big wooden
bin stored down
in our cold room
that fed us all through
raw dark winters
and long into spring—
what grew me
wise enough
to know the moon
would never stay
put in our old pine
nor even inside me.

Mother goes to the underworld

Our kitchen slants, empty.
Flies buzz from the fields,
big black ones with green prisms
for eyes. They land on counters
and scoot across like miniature
rodents, so busy. At the dirty
window, they cry louder
looking for some way out.
A sticky, brown fly strip
waves gracefully from the ceiling
dancing in the warm air.

I want my mother in her red
striped apron, a muslin dishtowel
wiping a drinking glass, or punching
down the dough. Today it is the kitchen
of not eating. Father comes
from the garden, spring harvest
in his dirt covered hands. Pleading,
he wants to know where she is.
What can I tell him?
She is in the underworld

refusing the earth's fruits.
No flaming torch, no
golden chariot can drag
her back. *You will abandon
her,* I think. *In your still
brown chair out back
with the dogs around you.*
And, later with your beer
at the Hotel bar, your sweaty
arms around another, while
I stay at this hearth, this home.

Letter to the bedroom window

After Tahereh Mafi, Shatter Me

I want to ask
what it meant to be

married to the moon.

Did it make you
wish to disappear

until she shifted

from wan to gleaming?
Did she leave you

cratered? Emptied—

in her absence.
I want to ask

if you were loyal,

what that meant
in her sometimes

dark moments.

Were you steadfast,
to different versions

of her face, uncertain

light streaming in
you, bedroom window?

You who thought

the moon was your
trusted companion

when instead

you were alone,
imperfect creation,

waiting for her beam

rising full as a pond
on the slim horizon

ready to rinse you

who felt forsaken,
clean, whole again.

When mother was illusionist

We gathered round her long limbs—
flurry that cast no shadows
scintillating through the house,

a kind of lightshow without fanfare,
but billow stirring up the maelstrom
just to capture its swirl of coal dust,

garden dirt, dog prints—daily eddy
contained in a dust cloth, rags she
tied onto our socks so we skated

across paste-waxed floors like small
circus clowns, grounded aerialists
looking for lift-off, flying machines

or ropes to climb out of the blue hills
that contained us. Mother, magician
bending to the moment, whichever

way so the show goes on—mess hall
chef, choreographer, clean-up crew.
When her magic failed, we turned

tinker, raised the big tent around us
and kept it staked to ground, fed
the feral cats and work horses, flew

circus flags so no one really knew
she had simply stopped believing.
Inside, our mechanisms all grew still.

Depression as guest

In a picnic Polaroid down on the farm, all of us wince
into the lemon light of May. The yard, new with green,

table laid with Tupperware. You can't see people much,
but here my sister peeks out next to the macaroni salad.

She's stuffed in near Granny, who's wearing pink and glasses
pointy as triangles. We carry out what was inside all winter.

Chairs, cabbage from the cold room—sliced thin,
folded into vinegar and Hellman's—fried chicken,

rhubarb cake, Wise chips. And Mom is there, isn't she?
The halo of her hair somewhere. Dad, too, in his tee shirt.

It's Memorial Day. We spent the morning in the garden
planting. It's celebration time after Grant took flowers

up to all the graves. And, somehow, this is when she comes
to holidays, D. who stands off to the side, planted there

like some odd tree. No one seems to question it. She
is morose, but she is family, so in she comes. And she

sits down. And, evermore, we add her in, her troubled
stare and rumpled clothes. She sleeps all day, then joins us.

For the special days. So, holidays will never be the same.
I understand it now. Along with joy, we have to think of her.

House flies

Maybe the flies come
when she sleeps,
window dwellers,
wringing their hands,
little holy ones.
In the kitchen, buzzing
in the key of F.
How could they believe –
praying or singing –
in the days of her
metamorphosis?
Looking for a warm place
for winter. It's probably
too late now. Like putting
a penny in a bag of water.
What will gather, what will
seep—on the table
on the porch screen?
In the springtime –
meat or molasses,
fruit or some sugar,
we had to choose.
What to serve for dinner,
what to use to bait the trap?

Recipe for a daughter leaving

After Jihyun Yun's "Reversal" and Carla Sofia Ferreira

Chop the salt pork into small squares like bits of your childhood. (When you ate what was slaughtered for you. As your mother emptied warm loaves onto those Formica countertops from dark thick tins.) Sprinkle the salt pork like small windows, like tiny mirrors, throughout the house. Retain some bits for cooking, like reminders, on top of the table where you will pour the dressing over the greens. Dressing, the leaking from your dad's heart. Add a dousing of vinegar to the grease in the pan. Stir to gather up all the scrapings, like the women before you—always twining a spatula around for good luck, good riddance. Remove the salt pork, crisp and cooling from the cast iron. Until you have a bowlful of leaves with spears. In early spring, when the dandelions first sprout, dig a basket of them for everyone, going or eventually gone.

Instructions on leaving {mother}

In order to leave her, you must find her
outside the kitchen window, pale, waning

where just days ago, she was here,
a perpetual streetlight beaming in,

crown of hickory and oak framing her.
Now she has bled again into daylight

dissolved into the gypsum bowl above—
translucent, thin enough to puncture

everything you thought you knew
about fixtures, solidity, timepieces.

Here you thought she was a wristwatch
you could plan a day around, regular

as an almanac, even with her phases.
Now, mother as floater moon, alabaster

searchlight over the tree line, suspended.
Soon the sun denudes the sky, obscures her.

But she has seeped outside now, oxygen.

The end of childhood

Your parents' tightened
lips, their narrow love—
how it tipped & tilted
like the summer Ferris wheel
all smoke & burnt candy.
You, leaning over the edge
to see it all—old ball field,
swirling night bats, dogs
& beer faced fathers. Where
is your mother? Gone, again?
That question slow burning,
but here the lights
are twinkly, everyone
is gathering, rippled
& holding something
spooled loosely –
giant blue bears, a pinwheel,
caramel apples on sticks, silvery
balloons hovering on the midway.
Empty in this moistness, you
circling around, swooping
& knotted, your stomach,
your sinking heart.

Killing the fish

I don't suppose he thought
about it much—the silver fish

we caught dumped in the plastic pail,
their slip and curl and gasp

when he poured them in the sink.
But I looked on at his steadiness,

how he took pliers to the skin
after he cut a thin circle round the head

and yanked it off like you undress a doll
with clothes too tight.

Likewise, he gutted them.
His fish knife held mirrored

scales in tiny patches on its shaft
until he washed them off.

The guts hauled to the garbage pile
or buried underneath the beans.

The filets tossed in flour and laid out
in a buttered pan for lunch.

The fish were mild in their death
and only spoke of pond and mud

and all that time held in their cold
green world. I ate them

like a tiny prayer, or maybe less
as if I knew violence

was part of everyday, what
I was given in my life.

Sack dress

Dad bought dog feed for his hounds in cloth sacks: sprinkled lemon daisies on a field of cotton polka dots. He mixed the meal in a gallon pail with hot tap water that smelled like metal, scraped the bottom with a big old restaurant spoon. Walked outside & dumped the mush in concrete dishes he made himself so they wouldn't tip. We saved the bags, still smelling of meat parts mixed with corn. Turned them inside out, washed & hung

them on the line until they gathered air enough to float away. Held on until they piled into stacks, then went to town for patterns at Laceyville Variety. We cut the bags into pieces for tiered peasant, empire-waist dresses just like in *Seventeen*. Sewed on Mom's old Singer, taking turns in her bedroom while loose thread, fabric scraps gathered on the dusty floor. Heat held in the room from the corn rows & noonday sun outside. Hemmed & pressed, we tried on dresses,

twirled in vanity mirrors not big enough to see our bodies filling in the spaces, tight bodice to flowing rows, yellow, green & blue. We wanted floppy hats, platform sandals, but had a field of flowers on our backs, sweet film of sweat gathering under the smooth cloth right below our breasts. We wore our dresses to church & school right before the weather changed. There were no concerts off Route 6. Wyalusing only had a bowling alley. Sometimes a date would drive us to the movies.

Jeans & halter tops were more in style. No one wore dresses to the Tastee Freez for cones. At dusk, we'd end up in a field somewhere with beer, but bugs would come. Dresses never made much sense. One summer night, my sister's old boyfriend asked me to go to Vestal to see *Yes*; I wore my dress. He drove us down a country road, sun going down, golden & round. He stopped the car, leaned over & slid his hand up my legs. I leaned into the hard door, clamping fabric tight like a closed blossom, thin, still.

Girl of prey

      Still a girl, thin clad, asleep
in a college dorm. Wolf stumbles
          through the door, wakes me, fumbling.

      Slight fawn under bracken cover, I bolt
awake. *What do you...who?* I flutter
          like an owl stirred up in branches

      meant for camouflage. Girl of prey then,
sprung from woodland coiled bough.
          Steel teeth, the trap wolf sets with his false words.

      Oh, oh, I thought... you were... Do you know
where...? As if wolf does not leave me barred—
          night's cage holding my saw-edged self.

      Instead of captive now, when light sinks down
and love caresses, my falcon heart jolts swift.
          I unfold my wings; spread my talons wide.

How to stay alive

Walking down
the path of almost
night, its syrup
just starting to beckon
sycamore-sticky
& swelling.

A dark star falls
shooting arrow-light
into the back of my head,
branch-tangle-sky.
Fists & drums,

air so angry,
honed bolt of
howyoustayalive.
I am on the ground
hawk-wet & who
knows if I'm bleeding

but the wild boy
has bound me
& filled himself
with lightningbolt
as if he borrowed
the last rays sinking

above the treeline.
And the crows know
sharp-screeching
this flinted wrong
below the slightly
twisted pines they

perch in.
But I soothe-talk
like a mother waving

her voice a bit,
a small flag
soft-reminding

the feral one
full of this jagged
light how he
will treat me
when he does
what he will do.

I am a flashlight
glow worm crawling
up from moss ground
to spread a message:
cleanupyourmess,
comehometodinner

or dowhatyourmomsays.
And he leaves
after he gets what
he wants, but
he does not kill me.

small map

It was spring, and all the blooming trees
talking to me as if I were a red bird,
as if I should float with them, and they would
keep me, hold me in their triangle of apple
limbs, fallen stone, thick creek water flowing
and bending around itself. I kept on walking,
retracing the same steps, and not getting found
or finding myself. As if I were trapped in a yellow-
white maze, no one to rescue me. My heart stuck
in its chamber, pounding out its empty rat-tat-tat,
rat-tat-tat. I am not of the place I live, my spot
on the darkened earth. As if I believed I could
get back there. Loss, this strange land I live in.
No god or whatever to recognize or find me.

The end of girlhood

After James Wright & Joni Mitchell

Just off the highway, scrub brush, cast-
off trash, thin trees blooming so abrupt.
Gash of common pear, serviceberry:
years I gave away my body in a rush.

What I could not tame with rationality,
tears & moons. Me, a Ferris wheel, wild
round thing swirling in the night, glowing
circle dance. Following with no apology.

At each stop, taking, discarding. Brazen
dreams & scheming, all the while looking
over my shoulder tossing salt, mourning
the soft give of June, not going home.

Hunting season

On a day of bone picked clean, scavengers
circling, worry rattling its deep hollow,
this path to wander down or plod even
if I don't belong in open air.

Leaf quilt, how woods build a room of gold
then paint it tawny or slick grey in late fall.
Clearings, songbird still, or whistling through
my chafing heart, softly waving phragmites.

Off the small ridge, roots entwine like steps
and I pick my way down—alone, except for
the dog who halts now and then, pricks
her velvet ears which stand like little tents.

Below, the breeze is damp off the farm pond.
Three fat swans float and dip.
Their bottoms rise like silent boat hulls, plump
and solid, while the heron skulks in the corner

where she often waits, a sheath, in shadow.
I salute her as I do the white bellied
hawk dangling a squirming small thing from her
beak, the huntress who'll protect and keep me.

After college

My dull metal sweater, heart poured open,
shallow as a narrow puddle—

I packed without it, left with the slightest
jacket full of feathers. Saw the flatlands,

prairie. Knew the bluestem there would keep me
rooted deep. How I could see a storm coming

from far off, longways into twilight. So
much time before rain came, I could get ready.

On my little porch in Kansas, I sat through
a thunderstorm to see what would happen.

Held on stubborn, shellacked and pelted.
Became a yellow thing and floated

overhead while the wind bore down and tried
to tear up all the furniture. I kept

on—wanting to believe in aftermaths.
Then settled back to earth, a summer bird

sinking into the garden. Back there singing
while the sky cleared up as if nothing

had really happened—the bumpy brick street
filled with shrapnel from the solitary elm.

Fourth of July

There was so much glare
at the fairgrounds—
coal sky stabbed with fire,
vaulted confetti, pulsing
thread-light extinguishing
so fast I was not quite sure
of its existence. Until the next
one blew, covering me
with temporary blossoms,
nothing left to hold on to.

When did I learn to not trust
light—flashing his hair,
even his shoes gave off a glow.
I shied away from his bold shine
into the practiced din of indoors,
cooped myself like a small chicken
for weeks until I craved
the yellow green of a backyard.
Like a stubborn garden,
untended, climbs toward sun.

How I learned to love Kansas

I found Sagitta, the Arrow, in the August night that year
not knowing if I needed freedom or revenge.

I watched the grasses, taller than me, swallow the sky.
Wished the Kaw River would ferry me somewhere.

I emptied myself of everything I thought I wanted
and waited to see what would fill me back up.

It's hard to remember what the heart wants when it tugs
like a jump rope. Sometimes you aren't paying attention.

It's hard to remember what happened after I saw him,
then tried to fall asleep in my sweltering summer bed.

I should have known Kansas can change directions—
the way thunderheads brewed miles away, then spilled

crazy like a thousand lawn sprinklers tipped and whirling,
drenching eaves and windows, turning into carwash.

He couldn't have known I wanted to go shoot pool again
at that bar on 6th Street, see if I could beat him at Centipede.

Watch the way his mouth curved into the smoky light
when he laughed, the steady move of his hands on the cue.

I was not sure how to fill my time—preparing the ground,
planting fall peas in sod along the back chain-link fence.

In the future, there will be days I take for granted.
In the future, seasons will slide by like the river.

What I didn't know is that this is how a life can start.
What I didn't know is that I would not be alone.

I stood on the edge of the Flint Hills and walked
into its swales until I felt like coming home

Midwest soil

I turn to loam
moving sedimentary
centuries out of my skin.
Our damp bed sinks
through moss leaf-litter
submerged as eons
of sweet grass
sweep oak
prairie canopy.
Spangled glint,
tulip poplar blooms
twisting in the wind.

Your body is clay
on creek bank.
Gasp of spring
slipping over
dimpled brook-rock.
Where woods touch
water, that edge—
luxuriant blurring.
Rasp and sedge.
Plunging to cool
low hanging
cedar swim hole.

August

Falls on a carpet
of hay, waist high,
corn above our heads,
roadside elderberry
ripening steadily.
Mourning doves
hoot from the roof.
Lush thoughts
overtake my
pragmatic self.
We should marry
before the winter comes.

Planted

When the date was scheduled, the time set,
I found the task inevitable, like opening
a closed door, or leaving a dark room, sun
through new leaves just beginning to unfold.
I wanted to cry in relief, but there was
no escape, really. That word, sin, confusing
me. What I knew was ultimately right.
Afterwards, we went to a café, ordered food.

I needed substance, so the waitress brought
roast beef, mashed potatoes, a vanilla shake.
With a nod, the older woman acknowledged
I must be pregnant. "It's ok, honey, that
queasy stomach won't last long." Your arm
around me, a temporary crutch. When we
got home, I slept, rested, but the next day
planted the whole garden in two hours flat.

Argument

When you stop talking, sharp lines etch across your forehead,
thin and endless, an interstate highway across Wyoming,

nothing in sight for miles. Your narrow lips disappear. A car
door slams in your eyes. Malevolent clouds tumble over Kansas,

fat and violet. Wanting a rest top with maps and picnic tables
but getting an old Gulf station. Two guys chewing tobacco

wave me to the back where mechanics share the bathroom.
This rueful swath of road, bad motels with thin sheets, no soap,

cold showers. Barns with broken slats that won't survive
the year. This is how distance begins. Our silent fields, lapped

by snow, ironed smooth as linen. Coarse stubble stretched in rows.
Endless hills. My transgressions. What you have to tell me, stark,

unspoken. A hawk's belly glinting like silver. Our differences clear
as February light. Somewhere down the road, there is a warm table,

somewhere a bed with quiet quilts, a small fire tamped down.
Readied for the long night.

Cleaning the shed

I want to clean something down to the bones.
Make a closed space open. Bring in air.
Let go of avarice. As if all that I have gathered
is now hidden from me, taken. Squirrel nests.
Stack of plastic buckets, holes chewed through.
Fluff filled flowerpots. Even the hammock rope.

Little candle house carried out into light. Sudden
flutter, glinting against thin filigree. Spicebush
swallowtail clings, black gloss wings, small orange-
blue moon dots on her tail. Hatched in the dark
spring. The shed's last and only captive, hesitating
even when she is shown an opening, a way home.

When you wish only for erasure, you disappear.
But when you empty a place, you can feel whole.
Before you anoint the axe handle, appoint bamboo
stakes to their corners, an inspector arrives—slender
milk snake, body ringed in gold, stretches her length
across the bottom beams, slides up the wall on her
way out. Swift flicker. Mouse-hunter. Omen.

II

Check stubs from the Super Duper

The summer Dad sold the house, we climbed the ladder
stair one last time and smelled the attic air, how sawdust

insulation baked in late July gave off a heat of honeybee
that felt old and dry and safe somehow, though sweat

gathered on our lips as we pored over crumbling boxes,
lamps and stacks of books. I wanted to find Mom up there

too, some evidence of her years spent in those stucco walls:
a crepe black suit with pants I ended up with that folded

lengthwise into creases like accordions, the faded ivory
tea dress she never wore with embroidered flowers

on the neck, an orange and yellow pillbox hat. Instead,
a pile of check stubs from the Super Duper, her flowing

script, the perfect penmanship she taught in elementary
school. All those trips to buy detergent, flour, yeast, I

wanted to keep them, confirmation of her dailiness,
the $14.53 in August '69. But when my sister scooped

them up and put them in the trash, I did not say a word.
Just promised to remember them, how lithe they seemed

and light, like her before she ended up, before she left
our home, before the end of ends, and no one there to shop

and cook and sort what stayed inside the house and what
we took up to the attic room to store for what came next.

Finding shore

Maybe the loggerhead turtles, like all of us,
rush to leave home no matter how unprepared,

using moon and starlight to find shore, floating
in undertow, sideways to the waves' crests. Once

during college, I hitched a night ride to Boston
on a meat truck with just a backpack to see Mom.

The driver dropped me way at the end
of the Orange line out in Jamaica Plain

where the semis swarmed the terminals.
Those turtles had to survive in open water

until they made it to the Gyre—sea current
flowing in a circle, a watery bed to protect them.

I listened carefully to the older women
going to work early on the train who told me where

to switch cars, perspiring quietly when they asked
what I was doing there at 6 in the morning. I don't

think I had traveled on the subway alone. The train car
full: face, face, face, window, swerving clanking metal,

brakes screeching. Only 1 in 4000 baby turtles reach
adulthood, and at first, they only swim a half mile

an hour. I knew the Blue Line enough, once I saw harbor
and planes taking off at Logan, to find my way toward

Maverick, past the hustlers and the buskers. I kept
going steadily, trying not to think about how the stair-

ways smelled, and why people had to sleep there any-
way. I was wishing to float in the Sargasso, somewhere

to hide while the turtles made their way thousands
of miles to northern inlets, where waves meet fresh

water, eating tiny crustaceans, eventually jelly fish
and hermit crab along the way. I bought a corn muffin.

The counterman grilled it like they did back then, slicing
it exactly in two halves, moons crisped brown with butter.

To find their way back home, loggerheads use the earth's
magnetic field—we don't know how—maybe an inherited

magnetic compass. I was never that good at directions,
but I went back and forth to Boston for the next dozen

years, curled on Mom's small couch in her basement
apartment near the vast deep sea.

Container of the world

I am the container of the world,
        the whole hull of a lake ship at port.
Morning fog is lifting off me

        steaming in my eagerness.
Winter's ice has not yet broken through
        even though it is spring, so waves

are frozen in mid-air. Everything
        is ready for me—opening in the smallest
of spaces, pockets like air bubbles in the ice.

        Pike and steelhead sluggish in waiting,
rocking in swaying currents
        like underwater babies,

the fluid of the blue-grey lake tumbling
        gently, the way hands cup eggs while
carrying them. As if that is all I want

        to hold in the giant maw of my belly—
that small safeness, a place of wonder,
        however murky and unready. This

holding, like breath, sharp, necessary.
        But cold, sour until filled, not
knowing if I ever will be.

First married

The river is slow to anger, almost stagnant in mid-summer. Smells like moss rock, the burbled slippery kind that turns rust brown in August, reeks of rotting. Moon still out, agrees to follow me, whittled under her constant orange eye. I am smoldering, newly furrowed. Trapped sparrow against heavy glass. Drowning in wallpaper, odor of his talcum, oiled bureau, while talons spring from my fingers. But nothing to spear except words which cannot be captured. Ice clouds, then fogbanks all round him seep inside me, stay like a sad song thawing my heart, but chipping me apart chink by chink. I am going to be chiseled, a hunk of old plaster, the house remodeled, sleek plastic, textured glass. But I am just a dirt girl, so crawl to the garden, smell the spice of tomatoes just climbing out of their cages.

River prayer

After Vievee Francis "Another Antipastoral" and for the Huron River

I want to put down what the river has awakened—hill-girl rock
sliding down the mountain, floating on a waterway that has always

been inside, passage slick and hidden. How could I ignore this
slipping, the ease of it? Blood pulse, just as underestimated. Look,

the heron is carving herself into foreground, her pause before
fierceness. We are just as prehistoric. See what we have forgotten—

body as oar, a boat's pathway, coursing. There is a way beyond us.
The water's edge, an invitation. I have river so much in my core,

its plunge and sweep like a sob ready to burst. Here, Joe Pye weed
waving pink fists. Curly eel grass sunk, spiraled. My heart—tuber

of duck potato in the silted muck, pickerelweed, spiked arrow, cattail
driven deep in my marrow. There, a solitary trumpeter swan drifts

separated, eventually gathering into a cloud bank, dusk coming on.

Girth

For years, I thought of my body as *wisp*
wisp, wisp. I could slide through anything,
wave to and fro like a frond, brief stem
or if left alone, fern, cosmos, incorporeal.
But when I found love or love I thought
would stay, I rooted thick like sunflowers
out in Kansas, sticky stalk that grips earth
then flares into fire. Maybe it was giving
birth or living in the Midwest—now I see
girth grounds, keeps me. Granny standing
solid in the flower garden, her gladiolas
like swords toward the summer trees.
My body is house, wood stacked against
a bad winter and all the gardens swollen
fat with whatever sweetness I can gather.

to mother is a strange equation

Is to   be present
              to present   your body
wholly   to   something   other
    than   work/pleasure/sensation
instead   a creation   begun

unseen   this cellular   hatching
        in blood-deep   crevasse
a being   spun fresh
       knotted   gossamer-thin   you
don't feel   its stirring.

To want   to write
      or dwell   in   moments
too tenuous   so   attenuated
      long   nights   fretting   full
of ponder   not focus

on others   instead   self
    preservation   for   what came
next/after   for which
    there is   no   preparation
time   a   false notion.

To *mother*   this new
      gambit   a joint   assent
off kilter   odd route
     or manner   a state
of being   finding   your

self in   then rearranging
          your   whole   body skin
this you   plus one
          no memory   what is
     before   this   only now.

Small jar

You came in spring, reluctant to leave
your container home, strange fluttering.
I first thought you were a berry nub
not made from wild limbs and galloped
blood, glint I knew from saw-toothed leaves
and dapple. Tiny space held your heft
blown into room, filled me like a bowl
until I overflowed with fruit, sweet
enough to haul a basket, woven
straw under an April moon. Promise
like a harvest meant to come. I closed
my eyes, summer hovered down the road.
My work, the hardest work I'd yet do—
let you go and keep the gleam of you.

Restoration

Here, clapboard houses spurt from cracking flagstone.
Our daughters' songs peal through the subdivision.
In the woods, shadowy berries just below the school.
We wonder where the blue needle dragonflies come from.
Was there a buried creek waterway? We buy a blowup pool.
Scatter sidewalk chalk like chaff. Watch how the sun climbs.

I have your limbs around me now. The children are sleeping
in their singing beds. Yesterday, a spade, turned-over sod.
So much gravel and clay, discarded in the seeking.
Maybe we are all searching. But there, three
striped marbles, twirled moons all in a row
laid there by some small child who believed in Martians.
The way a tiny turquoise egg lands whole on hard concrete.

Preparing

Raking leaves at dusk, uncovering spring.
Started yesterday, but the rain came on.
Streetlights, those two persistent stars,
keep shining. Over the rise, all the weary
cars going on and on. Yesterday, a man
walked by the garden fence, picked up
a painted stone the girls tucked there.
Gazed at it, moving it round in his palm,
like something priceless. I swallowed
stones before I slept, and all night sank
into a future too heavy to carry. How do you
keep stones from sinking like that, I wonder?
How do you hold the wild shoots
of spring inside you, instead?

Tethering

I am sorry, she told me—about her skin, apple red baked in a summer sun. As if she had done something to me. As if it belonged to both of us, her covering, tethering from the world of cells. What her skin had become, disconnected from me. What she meant was, she had not been careful. What she meant—I was not part of her anymore. This loosening beyond touch.

I remember carrying her before I knew her. Frightened at the start to imagine who or what she was. This dream, only me witnessing, seaweed twisting in a watery cave, hollow, wispy. Tentacles rising from somewhere, fingers, legs. Skin inside the sac of me. The bulge of her, floating oblong, unbound, but fettered. As if the message hung there from the start—cocoon, hatch. Release.

{plastic}

I have never been a temporary mother, but there were days
I gave away my skin like wind fluff, fly away, drifting over fields

with no destination, only a thin layer over me, curtain flutter,
window-gauze I could see through. O to be pliable, able to make-

shift, even cast off without care, but left to cover if (in order to
secure) protection is warranted. Not this membrane, fog settling

in like a dew-cloud, suffocating. Maybe this is how depression took
my mother, cloaked her in Saran until she could not even recognize

herself. Before she knew what to do, film over her eyes, throat &
nose blocking out her children, dogs & house, man she loved, until

all she could see were the edges, pauses in between, plastic blotting
out full image. Nothing felt clear, stripped of all she had ever known,

plastic killing her, pretending to keep her safe, pristine & untouched
when instead she became a museum, mother who used to be, now

mummified under-layer, however visible, supposedly supple, but
smothered & still, wrapped up tight, secure & permanently gone.

Dissolution

Tiny night moths jumble, twirl on the wet lawn
like children who won't go to bed.
They sing out of the darkened quack grass,
flit about my feet until the dog yips,
bounds after them—endless dizzy circles
in the midnight cul-de-sac streetlight air.
I don't believe in magic anymore,
but I want to lie down among them,
rising out of the ground—small specters
cool and white, bringing me back to earth.

Days slip beneath my fingers, dribbles gone
with nothing to show. A full moon rises
over the dark soccer field, coyotes howl
in the woods, but I am viscous, flowing,
ghost stream seeping under the boulevard
whose essence no one sees or remembers
on my way to the Sister Lakes. Brother
lamp post, how will I find my way? Asphalt
blanket to warm me, slow channel below
in the storm sewers, raccoons by my feet.

I smell the end of summer, bruised mint,
gangly fennel crowns rising to face stars
I never gaze at anymore. So many
places I could root, but winter hurries
me. Slide into streambeds, swift as swallows
dipping for supper. Lyrical crickets
are chiming from the green beans: joy, joy!
But these children here in the grass, what can
be done for them? They are losing me now
like the sycamore whose perfume remains

long after the nighttime walk, silvery
trunk luminous, mottled bark stripped bare.
I cannot help myself. Once I was grass,
and the field held me. No matter how far
I walked, I could always come back home.
Now, the river is my hair, my body—

tributaries spreading mercurial
under the subdivision. I am whole,
a watershed. I have given up solidity.

Black walnuts

In the still air of a house, the nut shrivels into itself—
the way hot air balloons collapse when they run out of breath.

Little kernel settling into folds, curves, wavy grooves
as if there is a tiny brain under its sage-yellow skin.

Up on the ball field, kids from the neighborhood have piled
a trough of them. As if Grandpa was still here collecting nuts

for winter—paying us to pick them up under the tree's spread
where nothing grows right. Maybe that is what was wrong with

Mom back on the hill. Trying to live under the black walnut
when everyone knows the vulnerable won't survive it.

She was a mountain laurel or rhododendron; did not belong
under the fierce tree's canopy. Mom stood on the stone

ledge reeling in the laundry, day after day, line attached
to the black walnut that looked out over the valley of corn.

Black walnuts smell like deep woods—sharp-oiled
pine needles on a hot day, an almost flammable

needled pitch that tipped me into reverence, the drift
and waft of a pastor's vestments, his dark waxed hair.

But to Mom, the tree was a trap, its toxins withering her.
After a while, she stopped going outside, disappeared,

wilting into the bedclothes while the biochemicals her own brain
produced sent her so deep, it took years to pull her back out.

Recipes for mothering

Yellow cake

It is the same thing, this cake of everyday. The cake of white flour. Cake of eggs and not even butter. Probably Crisco, this cake. It is the cake of your mother, your grandmother when they were tired and spent. It is cake, but not the frosting. Nothing special, only cake because they told us we could have cake. Here is the dessert you were promised. Some salt, some baking powder. Not even vanilla if it is too expensive because your mom hates the fake kind. Maybe some almond flavoring because it's cheaper. Maybe she forgot to grease the pan, that kind of cake. Maybe you must chisel the cake out, but still, it's cake. Here it is. For you.

Meringue

You think this is the answer to your prayers, this covering. It changes the landscape—as if you created a mountain, a seascape of frozen wave, of joy. Oh glory, dewdrops of ice! A child's dream, this sledding down peaks. And, yet, such mystery, this creation. Such beauty your hands make. As if the baker is the always mother, full of life. Or defeat if she beats it too much. Out of duty, determination. Flattened. Such is the dilemma of daily purveyance.

Jam

Always this gathering, containment of worry. What the women before you gave you. A way to make something out of waste, out of too much. Tumult and tangle. A hedge of berries, overgrown. Finches and titmouse flitting, robins and jays eyeing you as if to say, get to it! A gravel roadside sweep, elderberries rise above. Pears about to sag in the old orchard, wasps circling. Take your sorrow and stew it down. Add sugar. Squirt a lemon for bitterness, to remember. Summer simmered, thin juice thickened, spread for winter.

Snow, the letting go

Today the snow is wandering
        over the backyard gate, fleeting.
Aimless as school out in June.
          Forgetting its purpose.

This is the secret of adolescence.
        It fills space completely—like snow.
When you leave it, you forget.
        But, here and now, it's called drifting,

a blizzard of momentary. A "what are you doing
        right now?" Each thought joining
on to the next. How snow caves form.
        Aren't they the best insulation?

The igloo of my daughter's mind. What room
        I can find her in, the place she calls
hers/not mine. I always thought the bricks
        were made of mud, or clay. Not river current,

able to freeze over, but always flowing underneath.
        No wonder I am always looking
out windows measuring snow. Wanting the covering.
        Entirely. However temporary.

The oldest daughter flies to Dublin

Over northern Canada, she may feel most alone,
although it is the longest day of the year

& the sun (diffuse or beacon-like) will follow
her over those low-slung mountains that go on

& on—boreal forest of larch, spruce, birch
spreading into bogs, fens, black marshy sponge

reflecting sky—pinprick of silver plane, no more
than a sliver, really, like the germ of an idea.

She will look out the plane window
& think of who lives down there, what other girl,

like her, is not sure, but goes on through her days
anyway, maybe surrounded by trees like woodland

caribou, shy & sturdy, that everyone will likely
one day depend upon. But for now, the other self,

the one her body houses full of this nebulous
wonder. I hope she feels like cloud then, weightless,

with what she sees below—that spread of nubby
canopy—at once factual & dreamlike.

While she, full at the same time of doubt & precision,
a shaft of thin sharp air, knifes her way through.

Here in the quiet Midwest

The women of suburbia water the lawn, the trees,
the flowers when July turns thatch to prairie stubble.

It is the least they can do. They are worried about growing
old, so they unleash themselves unto the spigot. Watching

themselves reflected in windows; they worry. What they
cannot clean, cannot spruce, cannot whittle away. Seeing

themselves in their progeny, who worry them, too, mothers'
hands worrying the dish cloth, the bed sheet. The next meal

they will wring from the worried faucet, the worried flame.
Their daughters worry about partners and money and babies.

What happens when worried dreams become just dreams.
Their fathers worry about what is broken and can't be fixed.

The worry of daughters facing a worried world. What girls
need out there. Whether to arm themselves. What to ferry

across state lines. What worry they will be left with after
leaving worry behind. In the quiet Midwest, neighbors

worry, too—about moths invading the cul-de-sac, about
no rain, the water bill, their dog who went lame, the son

who is leaving, this time maybe for good. This time maybe
they will only worry when he finally drives away, worry

following him until soybeans hit scrub, thinning, thinning.

Daughters leaving home in an age of aggression

Outside the night window, cicadas call—or tree frogs—
I never seem to remember which small thing. Soft
warning, this seething settling around the house. Racket
loud as the cars on the freeway at rush hour. Now calm

somehow, as if the grass was gossiping a bit, rustling
& whispering: What is happening in the subdivision?
Neighborhood news from the elementary school erupts—
young parents wondering which teacher their children

will have? What old silver & shoes someone gently lays
on the sidewalk berm, as if to say they've walked away.
Our small, privileged tragedies. When I pull warm
sheets from the dryer, the fabric still smells of their skin.

How much of a miracle—girls' cells remaining
wrapped up in fibers of cloth. The basement floor
cool beneath stored boxes, spread out like Lincoln logs
splayed– these filled with blue plastic plates, opaque

glasses, college texts, twin sheets twining round what is left
behind. How to let them go into this world of the strong-
armed? Their grandpa & his rifles like nostalgia,
how he taught us to hunt, but fear each other, watch

out for ourselves, not let there be a savior. Now,
a woman still seems like fresh meat. The word jackal
too good, coyotes too monogamous for such human beasts.
Commerce. Stripped blood & bone.

I listen too much, as if the wind had a scent
I could follow—as if I knew how to track
my daughters out there in the world—this place
of twisted facts, rabid dog eat dog, aggression

gone haywire. We've taught them to trust, but every time
choppers lift above the tree line here whirring in a rush,
headed for the hospital emergency route, I think of war.
Do I tell them—Prepare to arm, or don't prepare?

Late raking

Night begins to fall, late November
and the leaves not yet raked. Debris collects.

Under the deck, squirrel bones, a furred tail,
bricks spilling down like an old creek bed.

In the backyard, snow smatter. Atop the fence,
seed fluff, tendrils of winter clematis.

(As if spring stays with us. As if each pistil
bloomed a girl running through leaves.

Child with rain for hair, new crown of copper
falling, falling—into the leaf pile, the worn hammock.)

Brown blooms of the Annabelle hydrangea, slick
imprint of tulip poplar like my father's hands

fading after a day's work, worrying
what is yet to do before winter comes.

It used to be, it used to be—harsh rasp
of each pull, a farmer's scythe racing darkness.

Through a window, the kitchen brightens,
squares hazy-yellow like the glow of the moon.

Yard now full of shadows. Muted roar of cars.
Almost like a river rushing if I tilt my head enough.

Wolf moon over M-14

A rush of trucks waterfalls
        the morning with a roar
                like whitewater rapids.

Meanwhile, the moon's gaze
        dogged through trees,
                limbs rooted in naked sky.

Once I heard coyotes
        call in Saginaw, knew
                that frigid grip of howl

and yip, opened raw
        echoed rounds.
                Here the Wolf moon

sticks fast over snowy roofs
        of sleeping houses.
                I wonder what our yonder

has become. Why we still
        hold on to this badge
                of yellow-gold in early air

while we keen to hear
        something calling us,
                yearning over the ridge,

even if we know
        there is really nowhere
                left to go.

Men I grew up with

I know they wake early
to feed the dogs, put the coffee on,
get ready for the chores
whether or not there are cows still
in the barn or even if the structure

that holds equipment is empty now,
the hill wind winding through it.
When they open the door to the day,
dark greets them like a friend.
I know the banked warmth

of their bodies as they walk out
to the truck knowing that winter
has come and the heat is on,
wood is stacked against the house.
They test the wind's direction

tip of a finger held up, wetted.
But somewhere there is fear, too.
It grips them inside. Their hearts
tense there in the early blue.
I know they think their guns will help,

their wives, kids, too. The dogs outside
who bay to be fed, bay when it's time
to head out to track coyote or bear.
But the restlessness does not abate.
Not with whiskey or beer or sleep.

They drive winding roads, past gas rigs,
past water trucks plowing steady down
the narrow blacktop roads. Somewhere
back in time, they heard those hymns
the grandparents used to sing

holding firm to the wooden pew. They
were too little to understand the verses.
They want to know Jericho, the promised land.
They want to cross the Jordan River.
I think the words come back now.

Coming home: carnival

After Patti Smith

Love makes the wheels go round—as in, your heart is a vehicle
conveyed through small towns, worn-out suitcase you drag, only
stopping at the fair for pickled eggs, magenta jar of luck & hope.
The Ferris wheel is broken down & all the lights look dim,
forsaken while you wander round the same dirt path. The clam
booth steams just like the sea—though you're in Pennsylvania.

The pie ladies are smiling from their perch which smells like pine.
It's been redone, still *lemon, apple, rhubarb*, they preach.
Renounce, renounce & have a slice. Because the night, because
you're home & you're redeemed. Beside the Swings you halt.
See someone you used to know; he is old, does not see you.

That chartreuse light of August glowed just beyond the ballfield
when you arrived. Now the hawkers at the candy apple stand
put on their lights & all the games draw in the younger crowd.
Pitch dimes in old glass jars, try to win back the family name.
Then the Ferris wheel begins to turn & soon the fireworks will
parachute chrysanthemums into the dark. One year when you

were young, you were stuck at the top with a boy you liked.
Kids ran with sparklers on the hill like bobbing fireflies.
Hello, hello, you want to shout. *Remember me?* But no one
yells. And no one comes to sit near you. The carnival man
jerks his finger. You are next. He clamps you down in metal.
You ride in huge moist circles, your heart lurching at the top.

Wolfhound

We'll prepare for winter now forever.
Bring the lambs & bags of hickory nuts, jugs
of syrup from the sugar maple. Tiny hammers, tiny
jars of currant jelly. Let's bring nostalgia & the fox-

hounds, if there's room. We had to leave the barn
behind, the mama sheep. Let them forage
in the back ravine while the war goes on. Maybe
they'll survive the bobcats & the bears. Granny

looks like Jesus now. Bring on her stewed tomatoes,
Dad's smoked fish. This spaceship's like our brother's
geodome & all he taught us for survival. Grandpa
still hoarding twist ties in the woodshed. God,

what holds the ship together, what it runs on.
Dad's jacket smells like woodsmoke. We still
sing hymns & lick the pie plate. Granny writes
a sermon for each day, delivers it for cast & crew

with doilies & lace curtains on the windows.
Where is our hearthstone? What hive is this?
Fields & woods out back, we're stuck with only
what we knew, not sure if we are wolf or hound.

God of dogs

After summoning, snatch of dream at dawn: mound of towels
from the bath, dog rubbed down as vigorous as before, but beneath
my hands she shrank almost to puppyhood, diminished, but whole.

Why couldn't I rejoice she was with me still? My mind focused
on loss. Panicked as if my movements would make her disappear.
How do you prepare for grief, I want to ask the god of dogs? How

to brace myself for that next shoal and not collide. Blade my hands
through water, its slow churn. Boat on the river and the water's down,
Dad says. It's low, the current so still we are barely moving. Yet there

we are, the yellow sky of not-yet-spring. Mom, near ninety, sits
in the shower, crows like a nestling when she is ready—for the soap,
the wash rag, time to suds her hair, to smooth it. Her mouth, open

for the worm, and me, mama bird, on the wing scooping bugs or fluff.
What to feed her, what to keep the nest—place of landing—soft.
Here, the old dog naps on her thick pad, narrow head, frosted muzzle

right between her paws. It is the rest I crave, for her, for Mom when
lunch is ending. I say time for a nap, setting the radio to a slow jazz
drawl, flicking off the light. Her hair, damp from toweling after

the shower, wanting to tuck her in, adjust the blanket on the couch.
Murmur some short prayer or story, maybe of spring: the dogs
giving birth, all the puppies, finding them in the coop, that sharp

peak of joy, their newness, waxy fresh foul beginning in the vast
rough world. I'll hold your hand to watch it all until you go to sleep.

How I want the road to you

Beached with late February snow
mapping the way home, hill-shorn

back where the barns were full,
all the cows giving milk

and you not gone underground—
your bed of flour-dusted sills,

all the sugar dissolved in petals
outside the open window. Mother,

here your face is dune-swept
smooth and still, opening

like the sky coming clear
on March days, sudden sun

bearing down—ardent
as if winter never happened.

Perhaps you have gone north
to your Atlantic Ocean

and rest there on its shore,
tidal as the pull toward moon.

Meanwhile the corrugated road
rises up to meet me, rusted

sheds tawny in the afternoon,
wild turkeys hooding the field

and the ditch roaring its way
along the asphalt melting

all that has thawed, loosened
and let go under the ice.

Skating

In the end, my mother raises her hands together toward sky
like a believer looking for grace, but maybe she is just making
sure she can still move them, little feather bundles released
to the evening, gathering in the snowy bowl of the juniper.

In the dark TV flicker, figure skaters strut onto the ice—
turning into cranes or herons jutting their limbs up toward
white pine or lengthwise, long docks reaching out into lake
or sea transfigured to gulls or pelicans in V shapes, spinning

and diving through the air. Mom sinks into bone beneath
the glare and I wonder if she sees the girl scraping violet
across ice, gathering plumes then bursting open until she
is iridescent purple martin floating down to eagle dropping

suddenly into swell and flow—pierced, talons, if need be.
Meanwhile, Mom is skating beyond earth, past the tree line,
horizon, scarlet-pink, what birds left, a wave of shadow
settled under wing, the eaves and in all the shrubbery—

cloistered, quiet, while she blades on and on, ice covered
river holding her. Where sky whittles away stray clouds
at dusk, opening up to another body, another place
of refuge, thin sickle moon like a pathway there.

My mother's arms, estuaries at winter's end

She is turning brackish in the borderland
where water coalesces, still flowing

from the hills, but gathering into herself
briny, tidal—a push/pull from this world

into the next. Alluvial, swirled with silt,
she has journeyed slowly downriver,

mussel beds sprawling in her wake.
I cannot join her at this junction

back to sea where she began. But I want
to tell her I would. She is thin as shad,

the same spots on her shoulders as she
too struggles to find her way past dams,

bridge abutments, the broad obstacles
of our human world. She will end

the way of the green-blossom pearlies,
like all small bivalves, the river

abandoning her finally, our industrial
longing not keeping her harbored. Here

her blood filtered along its way, slowing,
now merging into sloughs or troughs

where she floats quietly in long shallows
while the waters flow opposite under,

above her, and she decides when to go.

Her last breath swishes grass

Here we are in the rye again—
tall grain above our heads
matted down to these nests
where we carve out space
for our tiny bodies' homes.

Calling her out there
near the back garden
to join us & she comes
of course, our young mother
drying her hands carefully,

leaving the hot rinse water
to let us show her what
we have done, what
we have created for her,
small worlds, green & round.

We say *Let's have egg
sandwiches & milky tea
out here!* when she visits,
pretend to be her—laugh-
light that spill-rushes the way

ditch water flows down
the bank below our stucco
house, churning, insistent
& overflowing from corn-
field on its long way to river.

In the pond before turning 65

My arms dive then float, exposed as bone
or ivory root in the pond's olive mud,
earthy milfoil carried into air by geese
arriving in the spring. Submerged fronds
ripple my limbs while I swim elongated
ovals near the edge lined with pine, maple, beech
where long ago sheep meadow hugged woods.
This is the place my mother rested after skating,
my little sister on her lap near Grandpa with his wool
flannel hat. An abandoned wooden raft is sinking

on the opposite bank, catty-corner
to the underwater boulder we always stood on,
children in the shallows where we felt powerful
and old. My hands flip in and out, little ghosts
in feeble light emanating from the burning sky.
I could be a sunfish wriggling in the cold green
but these phases of the July moon trail me instead
where I see my mother now that she has risen—
discreet, solitary, ready to disperse.

About the Author

Ellen Stone was born in Syracuse, NY, and grew up on Spring Hill in Pennsylvania's Appalachian Mountains above the north branch of the Susquehanna River. She received a B.A. from Antioch College and an M.S. from Kansas State University.

Ellen lives in Ann Arbor, Michigan, where she raised three daughters with her husband, Roger Lauer. She taught special education in Ann Arbor Public Schools from kindergarten to high school from 1986 until she retired in 2018. Ellen continues to advise a poetry club at Community High School where she taught for over 20 years. She is a co-host for a poetry monthly series, Skazat! and a co-editor for the literary journal, *Public School Poetry*.

Ellen's collection, *What Is in the Blood* was published by Mayapple Press in 2020. Her chapbook, *The Solid Living World* won the 2013 Michigan Writers Cooperative Press Chapbook Contest. Ellen's poems have appeared or are forthcoming in *Third Coast, Passages North, Michigan Quarterly Review Mixtape, Sweet Lit, The Museum of Americana, Great Lakes Review* and *Dunes Review,* among other places. Her poetry has been nominated multiple times for both the Pushcart Prize and Best of the Net. Ellen was a 2024 Good Hart Artist-in-Residence. Reach Ellen at www.ellenstone.org.

Notes

p.20-21—Some of the language in "Letter to a bedroom window" is borrowed from a quote by Tahereh Mafi, author of *Shatter Me*.
"The moon is a loyal companion. It never leaves. It's always there, watching, steadfast, knowing us in our light and dark moments, changing forever just as we do. Every day it's a different version of itself. Sometimes weak and wan, sometimes strong and full of light. The moon understands what it means to be human. Uncertain. Alone. Cratered by imperfections."

p.68-69—"Daughters leaving home in an age of aggression" was written during the 45th president's years in office. It alludes to a time of unrest and uncertainty for all vulnerable groups of American citizens but highlights a concern about women's safety.

p.70—Wolf moon over M-14" refers to "Saginaw "as Saginaw Forest, (a tract of forest owned by the University of Michigan), not the city of Saginaw.

p.75—"Wolfhound" was written at the beginning of the Covid pandemic in a 2020 and imagines a Noah's ark-like spaceship protecting my family of origin.

p.79—The name "green-blossom pearlies" in "My mother's arms, estuaries at river's end" is a reference to green-blossom pearly mussels, an endangered freshwater mussel native to the southern Appalachian Mountains in the eastern U.S.

Thank you

Here are the people I am indebted to:

My friends who read this manuscript and offered suggestions: Judith DeWoskin, Karen Holman, Carrie Strand Tebeau, Onna Solomon, Julie Babcock, Jennifer Metsker, Sarah Messer and Ruth Moscow Cohen.

My Skazat! poetry series co-hosts Scott Beal and Karrie Waarala, our participants and featured readers.

My wonderful writing group: Onna Solomon, Rachel Nelson, Katie Hartsock, Betsy Martinez, Adina Schoem, and Robyn Anspach.

My Community High School family including all the talented students in Poetry Club, and my colleagues still teaching, or now retired.

My writer friends and colleagues: Monica Rico, Ashwini Bhasi, Alison Swan, Sarah Messer, Keith Taylor (and wife, Christine Golus), Zilka Joseph, Jennifer Metsker, Tracy Anderson, Molly Raynor, Jason Crawford, and Karen Holman.

My up-north Michigan writer friends including, Teresa Scollon, Anne Marie Oomen, Jen Sperry Steinorth, Kris Kunz, David Hornibrook, James McCullough, and Carrie Strand Tebeau.

The organizations that support me: Bear River Writers' Conference with director, Cody Walker, Polly Rosenwaike, and the amazing faculty I have studied with for years; Good Hart Artist Residency and Sue and Bill Klco for the opportunity to write in one of the most beautiful places I know. Booksweet Bookstore for always saying yes.

My editor, Judith Kerman for believing in this book from the first few pages.

My friend, painter, Karin Wagner Coron for "Pennsylvania moon," that graces my book's cover.

My family in Pennsylvania and elsewhere who read all my work.

My dad who taught me to love the earth, as well as literature.

My mom, for everything.

My beloved husband, Roger and our daughters, my light, Rebekah, Clare and Abby.

Recent Titles from Mayapple Press...

Joy Gaines-Friedler, *Secular Audacity*, 2025
    Paper, 66pp, $21.95
    ISBN: 978-1-952781-26-1

Lisken Van Pelt Dus, *How Many Hands to Home*, 2025
    Paper, 78pp, $20.95
    ISBN: 978-1-952781-23-0

David Michael Nixon, *A Wolf Comes to My Window*, 2024
    Paper, 40pp, $18.95
    ISBN: 978-1-952781-22-3

Zilka Joseph, *Sweet Melida*, 2024
    Paper, 60pp, $19.95
    ISBN: 978-1-952781-19-3

Eleanor Lerman, *Slim Blue Universe*, 2024
    Paper, 68pp, $20.95
    ISBN: 978-1-982781-17-9

Cati Porter, *Small Mammals*, 2023
    Paper, 78pp, $19.94 plus s&h
    ISBN 978-1-952781-15-5

Eleanor Lerman, *The Game Cafe*, 2022
    Paper, 160pp, $22.95 plus s&h
    ISBN 978-1-952781-13-1

Goria Nixon-John, *The Dark Safekeeping*, 2022
    Paper, 92pp, $19.85 plus s&h
    ISBN: 978-1-952781-11-7

Nancy Takacs, *Dearest Water*, 2022
    Paper, 84pp, $19.95 plus s&h
    ISBN: 978-1-952781-09-4

Zilka Joseph, *In Our Beautiful Bones*, 2021
    Paper, 108pp, $19.95 plus s&h
    ISBN: 9780-1-952781-07-0

Ricardo Jesús Mejías Hernández, tr. Don Cellini,
Libro de Percances / Book of Mishaps, 2021
    Paper, 56pp, $18.95 plus s&h
    ISBN: 978-952781-05-6

For a complete catalog of Mayapple Press publications, please visit our website at *mayapplepress.com*. Books can be ordered direct from our website with secure on-line payment using PayPal, or by mail (check or money order). Or order through your local bookseller.